THE HUNT FOR OSAMA BIN LADEN

BY VALERIE BODDEN

CREATIVE EDUCATION • CREATIVE PAPERBACKS

Published by Creative Education and Creative Paperbacks
P.O. Box 227, Mankato, Minnesota 56002
Creative Education and Creative Paperbacks are imprints of
The Creative Company
www.thecreativecompany.us

Design by The Design Lab
Production by Colin O'Dea
Art direction by Rita Marshall
Printed in China

Photographs by 123RF (Erik Lattwein, Carolina K. Smith, M.D., zabelin),
Alamy (AF archive, Asianet-Pakistan, dpa picture alliance, Entertainment
Pictures), Corbis (David Howells, Reuters), Creative Commons Wikimedia
(9/11 Photos on Visual Hunt/Flickr, Petty Officer 1st Class Daniel Gay/
DVIDS, SAC Tim Laurence/Defence Imagery, Marines/United States Marine
Corps Official/Flickr, Hamid Mir, Hamid Mir/Canada Free Press, Mysid
[SVG]/United States Department of Defense, Official White House Photo
by Lawrence Jackson/Executive Office of the President of the United States,
CHIEF JOURNALIST S.A. THORNBLOOM/DIMOC, U.S. Navy photo by
Chief Photographer's Mate Johnny Bivera/United States Navy), Getty Images
(DigitalGlobe, MAHMUD HAMS/Stringer/AFP, Joe Raedle/Getty Images
News, Universal Images Group), iStockphoto (christophe_cerisier, guvendemir),
Shutterstock (Prazis Images)

Library of Congress Cataloging-in-Publication Data
Names: Bodden, Valerie, author.
Title: The hunt for Osama bin Laden / Valerie Bodden.
Series: Turning points.
Includes bibliographical references and index.
Summary: A historical account of the manhunt for Osama bin Laden, including
the events leading up to his death in 2011, the people involved, and the ways
al Qaeda and other terrorist groups have changed modern warfare.
Identifiers: ISBN 978-1-64026-175-4 (hardcover) / ISBN 978-1-62832-738-0
(pbk) / ISBN 978-1-64000-293-7 (eBook)
This title has been submitted for CIP processing under LCCN 2019935430.

CCSS: RI.5.1, 2, 3, 8; RI. 6.1, 2, 4, 7; RH.6–8.3, 4, 5, 6, 7, 8

First Edition HC 9 8 7 6 5 4 3 2 1
First Edition PBK 9 8 7 6 5 4 3 2 1

TABLE *of* CONTENTS

Fifty-six minutes after United Airlines Flight 175 struck the South Tower, the skyscraper collapsed, and speculation quickly turned toward Osama bin Laden and al Qaeda.

People around the world watched in horror on the morning of September 11, 2001, as television stations reported on the deadliest terrorist attack in modern history. Terrorists had flown two planes into the "Twin Towers" of the World Trade Center in New York City. They had crashed another plane into the **Pentagon** in Washington, D.C. A fourth plane, believed to be targeting the United States Capitol, crashed into a field in Shanksville, Pennsylvania. As the death toll mounted to nearly 3,000, the world wondered who could have carried out such an attack.

But officers at the Central Intelligence Agency (CIA) already had a suspect. For years, they had been keeping an eye on Osama bin Laden, the founder of a terrorist network known as al Qaeda. Only three years earlier, bin Laden had openly declared jihad, or holy war, on the U.S. Up until that September day in 2001, however, no one knew exactly what bin Laden and al Qaeda were capable of.

The September 11 bombings set off one of the most intense manhunts in U.S. history. Ultimately, that search would take 10 years and cost billions of dollars. But when U.S. Special Forces finally killed bin Laden on May 1, 2011, many around the world claimed that all the time and effort were worth it. Although bin Laden's death did not end the threat of terrorism, it did provide a sense of closure to many who had been affected by the September 11 attacks, making it a significant turning point in U.S. history.

Afghanistan's capital of Kabul is an ancient city that has seen several periods of strife, such as the Soviet occupation that began with the killing of the Afghan president in 1978.

CHAPTER ONE

MOST WANTED

The man who would one day become the world's most wanted terrorist grew up in Saudi Arabia, the son of a millionaire. After a relatively normal childhood, bin Laden was introduced to the works of **Islamist** leaders while attending King Abdul Aziz University in Saudi Arabia. These leaders called for the full implementation of **sharia** throughout **Muslim** countries. In the 1980s, bin Laden took up the Islamist cause, moving to Afghanistan to join jihadi fighters resisting a Soviet invasion there.

During the war, bin Laden established training bases across Afghanistan. At the bases, fighters learned to use assault rifles and explosives. They were also convinced of the need for jihad to overthrow non-Muslim governments. After the Afghan war ended with Soviet defeat in 1988, bin Laden established a new organization, which became known as al Qaeda ("the base"). Al Qaeda's stated goal was "to lift the word of God, to make His religion victorious."

Osama bin Laden

As al Qaeda expanded, young men from across the Middle East attended its training camps. Most saw bin Laden as a hero for turning away from a life of luxury to fight a holy war. Members closest to bin Laden swore *bayat*, or an oath of loyalty, to him. Many would have willingly given their lives for him.

In 1991, bin Laden moved to Sudan, where he established new al Qaeda training bases. Al Qaeda carried out its first attack in 1992, when operatives detonated a bomb at the Goldmohur Hotel in Aden, Yemen. Three U.S. soldiers staying at the hotel were killed. The next year, al Qaeda–trained terrorist Ramzi Yousef detonated a bomb in the World Trade Center in New York. Six people were killed and nearly 1,000 were injured. Later in the year, al Qaeda members trained Somali fighters to resist American forces arriving in Somalia as part of a United Nations (UN) aid mission. The fighters managed to down two Black Hawk helicopters, causing American forces to withdraw. This affirmed bin Laden's belief that the U.S. was weak. "Our boys were shocked by the low morale of the American soldier," he said, "and they realized that the American soldier was just a paper tiger." In 1995, al Qaeda bombed a military base in Saudi Arabia, killing five people, including three Americans.

By now, bin Laden had caught the attention

To combat the spread of terrorist organizations' influence in Afghanistan, American and Afghani forces worked—and prayed—together.

of the American intelligence community. But the extent of his involvement in such attacks remained unclear. In 1995, the CIA created the bin Laden unit. Counterterrorism specialists were tasked with tracking bin Laden's background and activities. Even so, the CIA didn't consider bin Laden its highest priority, especially after he was expelled from Sudan in May 1996. Bin Laden moved back to Afghanistan, which had descended into civil war. A group known as the **Taliban** controlled large parts of the country. It welcomed bin Laden and al Qaeda. In Afghanistan, bin Laden rose to the height of his power. By now, the al Qaeda

POINTING OUT

A LIKEABLE LEADER

Bin Laden's followers within al Qaeda saw him as both a military leader and as a father figure. Many called him Sheikh ("chief") or uncle. According to those who knew him best, bin Laden was likeable. "Bin Laden [was] a very charismatic person who could persuade people simply by his way of talking," said Shadi Adalla, one of bin Laden's personal bodyguards. "One could say that he 'seduced' many young men." After interviewing bin Laden, British journalist Abdel Bari Atwan agreed, "the man is likeable. He is really nice…. He was extremely natural, very simple, very humble, and soft-spoken…. And he was a very good listener."

A decade after bin Laden's call for jihad, militant forces continued to train openly in unstable areas of the Middle East such as the Gaza Strip.

leader had decided that America was his number-one enemy. According to journalist Peter Bergen, bin Laden felt the U.S. "propped up the godless dictatorships and monarchies of the Middle East and, of course, Israel." Bin Laden resented the presence of U.S. troops anywhere in the Arabian peninsula or what had traditionally been Arab-held lands.

In 1996, bin Laden called for jihad against America. He began to grant media interviews, seeking publicity for his cause. Although bin Laden spoke softly, his tone conveyed a deep hatred for the West. He warned, "What you people in the West simply don't understand is that we love death even more than [you] love life." In 1998, bin Laden went even farther and issued a *fatwa*, or religious document, declaring war on the U.S. He said it was the duty of "every Muslim who believes in Allah to do Allah's will by killing Americans and stealing their money wherever and whenever possible."

The U.S. intelligence community took bin Laden's threats seriously. The bin Laden unit at the CIA spent long days sorting through intelligence, trying to figure out where bin Laden would strike. But they didn't have enough specific information. On August 7, 1998, al Qaeda bombed the U.S. **embassies** in Nairobi, Kenya, and Dar es Salaam, Tanzania. They killed nearly 250 and injured more than 5,000.

In response, the U.S. hit known al Qaeda camps in Afghanistan with cruise missiles. Although the missiles killed some terrorist leaders, bin Laden survived. His reputation soared. New recruits flooded into al Qaeda training camps. Over the coming years, the U.S. continued to look for ways to capture or kill bin Laden. One plan involved using Afghan allies to snatch him from his home at night. On other occasions, additional missile strikes were considered. But each time, the plan was rejected. An outright attack might result in civilian casualties. Another miss could elevate bin Laden's status even more. Some within the intelligence community thought it was worth taking such risks to stop bin Laden. "We may well come to regret the decision not to go ahead," CIA field agent Gary Schroen wrote after one scrapped mission to capture the terrorist.

Meanwhile, fears of another, even worse attack grew. On October 12, 2000, al Qaeda operatives pulled a small boat alongside the massive U.S. Navy destroyer USS *Cole*. They detonated explosives, ripping a hole in the side of the *Cole* and killing 17 sailors. Anticipating retaliation, bin Laden moved to a new house each night. But retaliation never came. Although the CIA could link the bombing to al Qaeda, it couldn't prove bin Laden's direct involvement.

Threat reports continued to increase throughout the spring and summer of 2001. Most seemed to indicate that the next attack would also be overseas. But on September 11, the terrorists struck on American soil. They killed 3,000 people as hijackers piloted planes into the World Trade Center in New York, the Pentagon in Washington, D.C., and a field in Shanksville, Pennsylvania. Addressing the

The term "ground zero" refers to a site of devastation and soon became synonymous with the area around the World Trade Center.

nation that afternoon, president George W. Bush declared, "Freedom itself was attacked this morning by a faceless coward, and freedom will be defended."

The attacker didn't remain faceless for long. The CIA was confident the attack had been carried out by bin Laden. On September 17, Bush signed a document authorizing the hunting down—and killing, if necessary—of al Qaeda leaders, including bin Laden. "I want justice," Bush said. "And there's an old poster out West, I recall, that said, 'Wanted, Dead or Alive.'"

POINTING OUT

CHILD MILLIONAIRE TO TERRORIST

Osama bin Laden was born in 1957, the 17th of 57 children born to Saudi millionaire Muhammad Awad bin Laden. His mother, Alia Ghanem, remembered her son as "a shy kid, very nice, very considerate." He enjoyed horseback riding, swimming, and hunting. Although his family had enough money to send him to a school in the West, bin Laden chose to attend King Abdul Aziz University in Saudi Arabia. Bin Laden studied business administration, but he was most fascinated by classes that introduced him to Islamist ideals and jihad. He dropped out of college and joined the jihad against the Soviet Union in Afghanistan.

CHAPTER TWO

SEEKING SHELTER

Bin Laden's last known whereabouts were in Afghanistan. Most in the U.S. intelligence community suspected he was still there, sheltered by the Taliban. President Bush called on the Taliban to turn bin Laden over to the U.S. He also called for a global war on terror, saying the U.S. would "make no distinction between the terrorists who committed these acts and those who harbor them." But Taliban leader **Mullah Omar** refused to turn over bin Laden. "Islam says that when a Muslim asks for shelter, give the shelter and never hand him over to the enemy," Omar said. "Osama has helped the jihad in Afghanistan, he was with us in bad days, and I am not going to give him to anyone."

On October 7, 2001, the U.S. launched **Operation Enduring Freedom** against the Taliban, bombing locations across Afghanistan. In addition, about 400 U.S. troops entered the country. Their job was to aid Afghanistan's main resistance group, the **Northern Alliance**, in its fight to overthrow the Taliban.

The same day the U.S. launched its attack, bin

George W. Bush

American forces deployed to Afghanistan encountered challenging terrain and conditions upon arrival in that mountainous and arid country.

Laden released a new video, probably taped some time earlier. In it, he said the 9/11 attacks were revenge for what the U.S. had done to the Arab world (the 22 countries connected by the Arabic language, culture, and history). "There is America, hit by God in one of its softest spots. Its greatest buildings were destroyed, thank God for that. There is America, full of fear from its north to its south, from its west to its east. Thank God for that. What America tastes now is something insignificant compared to what we have tasted for scores of years."

Despite bin Laden's boasts, the U.S. and

POINTING OUT

FOILED ATTEMPTS

As intelligence analysts searched for bin Laden, they also worked to prevent additional attacks. In late 2001, U.S. forces stopped a plot to attack embassies in the Philippines. In 2006, British police prevented an al Qaeda plot to blow up passenger jets. On September 11, 2009, police in New York arrested an al Qaeda–trained operative who planned to detonate bombs made with hair bleach. On Christmas Day 2009, passengers on a plane from Amsterdam to Detroit subdued a terrorist before the bomb he carried detonated. In 2010, al Qaeda tried to take down planes with bombs hidden in printer toner cartridges. But the bombs were discovered before the planes took off.

In December 2001, CIA operatives found an al Qaeda radio that was broadcasting bin Laden's speeches—it indicated that he was near Tora Bora.

17

After previous bombing runs that sealed shut cave entrances, forces had to use more explosives to reopen them in order to continue their search.

Northern Alliance quickly overpowered the Taliban. By November 12, the Afghan capital of Kabul had fallen to the Northern Alliance. The Taliban no longer had control of the country. The U.S. managed to capture or kill several known al Qaeda leaders. But bin Laden remained at large. In late November 2001, however, the CIA received intelligence that bin Laden had retreated to Tora Bora, a cave system in the mountains along the Afghanistan–Pakistan border. During the war with the Soviet Union, he had established a stronghold here. A small group of U.S. forces and Afghan fighters moved in to prepare for battle. On December 3, American planes began dropping thousands of pounds of bombs on Tora Bora. Bombing continued for the next two weeks. Forces on the ground engaged al Qaeda fighters outside the caves. The CIA estimated that 1,500 to 3,000 al Qaeda fighters had holed up in the cave system. From intercepted radio communications, they knew bin Laden was among them. They thought they had him trapped.

In mid-December, U.S. forces intercepted a radio communication in which bin Laden told his fighters they had his blessing to surrender. Many did so. Since bin Laden had expressed a desire to be **martyred** on numerous occasions, experts thought he was preparing to make his last stand.

Instead, bin Laden disappeared. Some thought this meant he had been killed in the airstrikes. But others figured the terrorist leader had managed to escape into the mountains behind Tora Bora, which led into Pakistan. American forces had not been stationed there. They had assumed that if bin Laden tried to escape, he would be captured by Pakistani forces.

For nearly a year, no one in the American intelligence community knew for certain if bin Laden was dead or alive. But in November 2002, the

Arabic-language news network Al Jazeera received an audiotape from bin Laden. On it, he spoke of world events that had occurred since the battle of Tora Bora, making it clear he was still alive.

The tape offered no clues about where bin Laden was, though. Several al Qaeda leaders had been captured in Pakistan. The CIA believed bin Laden was likely in that country. They thought he might be hiding in the Federally Administered Tribal Areas (FATA), a region in northwestern Pakistan where the federal government had minimal oversight.

Even as the U.S. searched for him, bin Laden

POINTING OUT

LOOKING FOR LEADS

Every time bin Laden released a new video, CIA officials scoured them, seeking clues to his location. "When there were videos, the highest priority was the background," according to bin Laden unit founder Michael Scheuer. "They didn't [care] about what he was talking about. If he was walking around, they would get geologists in and see if those rocks were particular to one place in Afghanistan." Experts analyzed birdsong and even plants in the videos to determine if they were unique to a specific location. Despite hours of analysis, none of the videos ever provided a solid lead on bin Laden's whereabouts.

Although they were originally developed more for surveillance than attack, Predator drones were outfitted with Hellfire missiles from 2001 on.

continued to put out videos and audiotapes calling for renewed attacks on the West. Al Qaeda operatives responded with attacks in Riyadh, Saudi Arabia, and Istanbul, Turkey, in 2003; Madrid, Spain, in 2004; and London, England, in 2005. Simultaneously, al Qaeda rebuilt, establishing new training camps in Pakistan. New, independent branches of the organization popped up in Iraq, Lebanon, Yemen, Somalia, and parts of North Africa.

By 2009, the U.S. was carrying out more than 45 **drone** strikes a year on al Qaeda targets in Afghanistan and Pakistan. A total of 30,000 U.S. troops were stationed in Afghanistan. Among them were the most elite Special Operations Forces in the U.S. military—the navy's Sea, Air, and Land Teams (SEALs) and the army's Delta Force. On almost a daily basis, these units carried out raids to capture or kill known al Qaeda members. But none of their raids targeted bin Laden—because no one knew where he was.

As they studied bin Laden's known habits and history, CIA officials realized he likely had at least some of his wives and children with him. This led them to theorize that bin Laden was likely in a Pakistani city. The CIA also gained a picture of bin Laden's communication network. Since the late 1990s, the al Qaeda leader had avoided using any electronic means of communication, including telephones or computers. He didn't

The 2012 movie Zero Dark Thirty covers the decade-long hunt for bin Laden and his death at the hands of an elite SEAL unit.

want his communications to be intercepted and tracked. Instead, he used a series of couriers to deliver his messages to al Qaeda operatives and to the media. Only the courier who worked directly with bin Laden ever saw him.

The CIA realized it needed to uncover the identity of this courier. Through interrogations of captured al Qaeda operatives, they learned that a man known as Abu Ahmed al-Kuwaiti was bin Laden's personal courier. In 2010, the CIA managed to track down al-Kuwaiti through his cell phone. They identified al-Kuwaiti's vehicle—a white Jeep with a spare tire on the back—and followed it to the city of Abbottabad. There it stopped at a large compound enclosed by a high fence. As one CIA official remembered, when he saw the compound he thought, "Holy Toledo! Who in al Qaeda would the group spend this kind of money on?" Agents hoped the answer might be the man they had spent nearly a decade looking for.

CHAPTER THREE

TAKING OUT A TERRORIST

Located only two hours by car from the Pakistani capital of Islamabad, Abbottabad was known as a safe, quiet city. It was also home to Pakistan's premier military training academy. It seemed an unlikely hideout for a terrorist leader.

But the CIA assembled a team to watch the compound. The roughly triangular-shaped plot was surrounded by 12-foot-high (3.7 m) walls topped by barbed wire. Inside the compound were two buildings—a three-story main house and a smaller guest house. The third floor of the main house had windows on only one side. And those windows were small, high, and blacked out. The floor opened onto a small terrace enclosed by a seven-foot-high (2.1 m) wall. The compound had no Internet or phone service. The residents— which included dozens of children—avoided their neighbors and burned their own trash.

Satellite imagery showed someone emerging from the main house every day. The figure walked around the compound's yard. But he remained in an area covered by a large tarp, so the satellites could never get a picture of more than his shadow. Still, many in the CIA began to suspect this mysterious walker was bin Laden. But they couldn't find a way to get inside the

As part of their training to capture bin Laden, the SEALs practiced fast-roping, a technique for landing in places where helicopters cannot touch down.

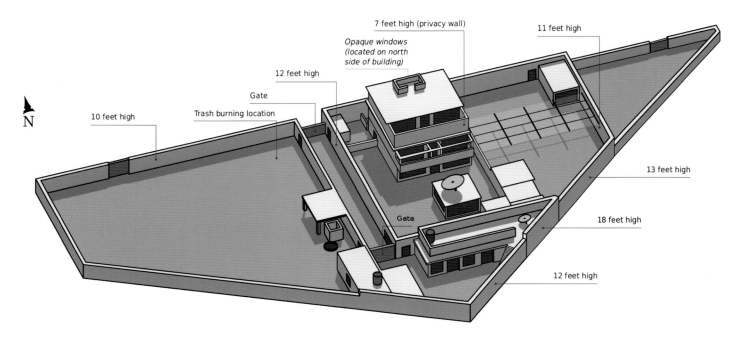

Planning for Operation Neptune Spear—the mission to hunt down bin Laden—took months of meticulous work by intelligence and military teams, especially as they plotted how best to breach the compound, based on surveillance materials.

compound to investigate further. They worried about accidentally spooking whoever was living there. If it was bin Laden, he might disappear again.

Even so, by November 2010, many of the lead bin Laden investigators were convinced he was in the compound. They took their information to U.S. president Barack Obama. Obama asked the CIA and Special Forces to give him options for action. In February 2011, they presented him with several possibilities. The first option was to plan a joint operation with the Pakistani military. But this plan was quickly discarded. Officials feared someone might tip off the compound's occupants. Another option was to strike the compound with drones or conventional bombs. But this would run the risk of accidently killing innocent civilians. In addition, bombs or drones could miss bin Laden. Even if they did hit him, there would be no way of obtaining **DNA** evidence to prove he was dead.

An assault by a small Special Forces team seemed to be the best option.

On April 26, 2011, 23 of the most experienced SEALs (plus a translator and a highly trained dog named Cairo) left for Bagram Airfield in Afghanistan. Even as the men were en route, debate over whether to launch the strike continued among the nation's leaders. Intelligence officials were 40 to 60 percent sure bin Laden was in the compound. To some, including vice president Joe Biden, that wasn't sure enough. Biden recommended holding off on the assault. Others said the intelligence would never get better. CIA director Leon Panetta made an impassioned case for moving forward with the attack. He told the president, "I've always used the test...: What would the average American say if he or she knew what we were talking about? And I think if you told the average American—we have the best intelligence we've had since Tora Bora, we have the chance to get the number-one terrorist in the world who attacked us on 9/11—I think they would say we've gotta go." On April 29, 2011, Obama gave the order to proceed with the raid.

Around 11:00 P.M. local time on the moonless night of May 1, 2011, two Black Hawk helicopters carrying the SEAL team took off from Jalalabad, Afghanistan. As they crossed the Pakistani border, the choppers flew fast and low to the ground. They had to avoid detection by Pakistani radar. Because the Pakistanis had not been informed of the raid, there was a danger that

Helicopters such as MH-60 Black Hawks (pictured) and Chinooks were used by the SEALs who went after bin Laden.

they might see the choppers as a threat and fire on them.

The seats had been removed from the choppers to save space. The men crammed onto the floor or sat on small camp stools for the hour-and-a-half flight. Some slept. Some tried to clear their minds. Others thought about the significance of what they were about to do. "Ever since the attacks, everyone in my line of work had dreamt of being involved in a mission like this," Navy SEAL Matt Bissonnette later wrote. "The al Qaeda leader personified everything we were fighting against."

As the choppers finally approached

POINTING OUT

SELF-IMPOSED CAPTIVITY

The intelligence collected from bin Laden's compound offered a picture of his life during the six years before his death. The terrorist leader had moved to Abbottabad with three of his wives and several of his children in 2005. Two more children were born during his time there. After moving to the compound, bin Laden rarely left the house except to walk around the covered yard. He spent his days praying, watching the news, reviewing his old videos, and writing. His writings showed he had never given up on the idea of striking America again. He especially hoped to do so as the 10-year anniversary of 9/11 approached.

Abbottabad, the operators readied for their mission. They were supposed to fast rope—or slide down ropes without safety harnesses—onto the roofs of the compound's buildings. But within moments, that plan was derailed. As the first chopper tried to cross the compound wall, it lost altitude, likely because of higher than expected temperatures. It went down. It crashed into the compound's courtyard nose-first.

None of the operators was hurt. And they were prepared for any **contingency**. They jumped from the crashed chopper and opened the compound's gate for the men from the second chopper, who had landed outside the compound

POINTING OUT

NO FIGHT

As the SEALs burst into his room, bin Laden didn't grab his guns to fight back. According to one SEAL, "bin Laden had more time to prepare than the others, yet he still didn't do anything. Did he believe his own message? Was he willing to fight the war he asked for? I don't think so. Otherwise, he would have at least gotten his gun and stood up for what he believed." Journalist Peter Bergen agreed that bin Laden seemed unprepared. "For all his bluster that he would go down fighting…, when the moment finally came, bin Laden went out not with a bang but with a whimper."

After bin Laden's death, Pakistan's government had the Abbottabad compound demolished.

after seeing the crash. Then they moved forward with their mission. One team cleared the guest house, killing al-Kuwaiti. Another team cleared the first floor of the main house. They killed al-Kuwaiti's brother Abrar and his wife.

Now the teams had to find their main target. On the second floor, they encountered bin Laden's 23-year-old son, Khalid. One operator shot him. Then, as the others continued searching the second floor, two SEALs moved up to the third-floor landing. A figure peered out of a room, then ducked back into it. The two SEALs quickly followed. A woman in the room launched herself in front of a tall figure, whom the men recognized as bin Laden. One of the operators shoved the woman aside and threw his body on top of hers, in case she was wearing a **suicide vest**. The other operator took aim and fired at bin Laden's chest and head. Brain matter spattered the floor and wall as the terrorist leader fell, dead. After examining the body, the SEALs radioed: "Geronimo, EKIA." (Geronimo was the code name they had given bin Laden. EKIA means "enemy killed in action.")

But the SEALs still had work to do. Some carried bin Laden's body to the helicopter. Others collected hard drives, DVDs, computer disks, and cell phones from the compound. The pilots of the downed helicopter set explosive charges to blow up the craft. They couldn't risk top-secret

U.S. Special Forces are some of the best-trained and most effective military units in the world—and many of their missions remain classified.

American **stealth** technology falling into anyone else's hands. A Chinook helicopter that had been stationed nearby arrived to pick up the team from the downed helicopter. Only 38 minutes after they had landed at the compound, the SEALs were on their way back to Afghanistan. They had accomplished their mission.

CHAPTER FOUR

CONTINUING THREATS

At 11:35 P.M. Eastern time on May 1, 2011, more than 55 million Americans watched as President Obama announced on live television: "Tonight I can report to the American people and to the world that the United States has conducted an operation that killed Osama bin Laden." In New York, Washington, D.C., and elsewhere, large crowds gathered to celebrate. Across the street from the White House, crowds at Lafayette Park sang the national anthem. In New York, people gathered where the Twin Towers had once stood, waving American flags and reciting the Pledge of Allegiance.

Benjamin Netanyahu

Leaders from around the world offered their congratulations. Israeli prime minister Benjamin Netanyahu called bin Laden's death "a resounding triumph for justice, freedom, and the values shared by all democratic nations fighting shoulder to shoulder in determination against terrorism." Italian foreign minister Franco Frattini said the operation was "a victory of good over evil, of justice over cruelty." Even many Muslim leaders expressed relief

Terrorist threats of today are not limited to those affiliated with al Qaeda or to other organizations in the Middle East and Africa.

IN LADEN

KILLED

A NATION CELEBRATES

...stice has been done

SPORTS SCORES INSIDE

LeBron James: Drives past Celtics' Rajon Rondo.
by Jeffrey M. Boan, AP

Celtics feel the heat
Miami leads Eastern Conference
...final with 99-90 win. NBA, 1, 10C

...Newsline

...NDAY, MAY 2, 2011

THE NATION'S NEWSPAPER

USA TODAY

A GANNETT COMPANY

Osama bin Lad...
dead, Obama s...

Jeff Bech...

U.S. forces tr...

BARACK OBAMA

BY JULIE PACE
AND MATT APUZZO
The Associated Press

WASHINGTON — Osama bin Laden,
the glowering mastermind behind
the Sept. 11, 2001, terror attacks
that killed thousands of Americans,
was slain Sunday in a firefight with
U.S. forces in Pakistan, ending a
manhunt that spanned a frustrating
decade.

"Justice has been done," President
Barack Obama said in a dramatic
late-night Sun-
day announce-
ment at the
White House.

A jubilant
crowd of thou-
sands gathered
outside the
White House as
word spread of
bin Laden's
death. Hundreds
more sang and
waved American
flags at Ground
Zero in New
York — where
the twin towers
that once stood
as symbols of
American eco-
nomic power
were brought
down by bin
Laden's hijack-
ers 10 years ago.
Another hi-

ONLINE

Video of
the celebra-
tion at the
Freedom
Bridge is
available
at www.
thenews
tribune.
com.

INSIDE

South
Sounders
and state
leaders
react to
Osama bin
Laden's
death.
See stories
back page

Pre...
killed him in a
targeted operation

By Jim Michaels
USA TODAY

WASHINGTON — Osama b...
mind behind the Sept. 1...
two wars, is dead...
Sunday.

"The Uni...
that h...

36

SEAL Team Six entered the media spotlight after the success of Operation Neptune Spear, which also inspired fictionalized accounts of the raid.

over bin Laden's death. Saudi deputy interior minister Prince Ahmed bin Abdulaziz said, "We hope that with the death of Osama bin Laden, an evil has ended. He has been an evil to himself, to his immediate family, and to the Arab countries."

As the world reacted to the news, bin Laden's body was being prepared for burial. Because they didn't want bin Laden's grave to become a shrine for other **extremists**, U.S. officials had decided to bury him at sea. His body was transported to the USS *Carl Vinson*. After being washed, wrapped, and prayed over, it was deposited into the Arabian Sea. Some Islamic scholars protested that burial

POINTING OUT

WATCHING FROM WASHINGTON

Throughout the raid on bin Laden's compound, a drone circling high above the city of Abbottabad sent live video footage to the U.S. There, Obama and his top advisers watched from a room at the White House. The room was quiet and tense. "I could almost hear heartbeats in the room," said intelligence official Robert Cardillo. Many of those watching were worried the whole house might be booby-trapped, as had been the case at several al Qaeda hideouts in Iraq. "I kept waiting for some big explosion from the house," said John Brennan, Obama's chief counterterrorism adviser. When the SEALs announced, "Geronimo, EKIA," Obama's reaction was a quiet, "We got him, we got him."

at sea was contrary to Islamic law. Other people around the world were outraged that bin Laden's body had not been displayed as proof he was dead. Although DNA samples taken from the body confirmed bin Laden's identity, conspiracy theories emerged that the U.S. had disposed of the body so quickly because it wasn't really bin Laden. Cindy Sheehan, a vocal antiwar activist, posted on Facebook, "I'm sorry, but if you believe the newest death of OBL [Osama bin Laden], you're stupid. Just think to yourself—they paraded [Iraqi leader] Saddam's dead sons around to prove they were dead—why do you suppose they hastily buried this version of OBL at sea?" Some believed Obama had faked bin Laden's death to improve his ratings approaching his re-election campaign. Other conspiracy theorists believed bin Laden had already been dead for years. They said the government was claiming to have killed him now so that the U.S. could justify invading Pakistan. Still others thought the U.S. wanted to use bin Laden's death as an excuse to pull military forces out of Afghanistan.

Despite such conspiracy theories, Obama refused to release photographs of the dead bin Laden. He cited fears the gory pictures would only inspire bin Laden's followers to retaliate. "The fact of the matter is," Obama told those who doubted the terrorist was dead, "you will not see bin Laden walking on this earth again."

Other organizations whom the U.S. identifies as terrorists, such as Pakistan's Jamaat-ud-Dawa, mourned bin Laden's death with public prayer services.

Even among those who believed that bin Laden had been killed in Abbottabad, there were doubts as to whether al Qaeda would continue to be as strong as ever. On May 6, 2011, al Qaeda released a statement promising retaliation. The organization said bin Laden's blood was "precious to us and to every Muslim…. We call upon our Muslim people in Pakistan, on whose land Sheikh Osama was killed, to rise up and revolt … to cleanse their country from the filth of the Americans who spread corruption in it." Within weeks of bin Laden's death, al Qaeda

POINTING OUT

A TEAM EFFORT

On May 6, 2011, President Obama met the SEAL team that had killed bin Laden. The president didn't ask who had taken the fatal shot—and the SEALs didn't volunteer that information. Instead, the SEAL commander said they had all played a role. "If you took one person out of the puzzle, we wouldn't have the competence to do the job we did; everybody's vital. It's not about the guy who pulled the trigger to kill bin Laden, it's about what we all did together." However, in 2013, Navy SEAL Robert O'Neill stepped forward and claimed to be the one who had taken the shots that killed bin Laden.

had named his longtime second-in-command, Ayman al-Zawahiri, as its new leader. Without bin Laden at the helm, however, al Qaeda seemed to flounder. By the first anniversary of bin Laden's death, many considered the organization a waning threat.

But new jihadist groups continued to arise, many of them related to or inspired by al Qaeda. Organizations such as Lashkar-e-Taiba in Pakistan, Al-Shabaab in Somalia, Boko Haram in Nigeria, and Ansaroul Islam in Burkina Faso spouted bin Laden's same extremist hatred. They carried out attacks in locations across Africa, Asia, and Europe.

To most world leaders, however, the greatest threat seemed to come from a new group known as the Islamic State of Iraq and the Levant (ISIL) or the Islamic State. Originally part of the al Qaeda network in Iraq, ISIL soon adopted tactics even more brutal than those of al Qaeda. Its leaders raped, tortured, and executed those who disobeyed its harsh laws. By 2014, ISIL had overrun large parts of Iraq and Syria and declared itself an Islamic **caliphate**. But by 2017, a U.S.-led **coalition** had managed to regain control of most of ISIL's territory. Even so, intelligence leaders warned that the group continued to pose a threat. Many Muslim extremists from the West had been recruited to fight for ISIL. As they returned to their homelands, they brought with

The 9/11 Memorial Plaza houses two reflecting pools within the footprints of the original Twin Towers of the World Trade Center.

them a new **ideology** and new fighting skills. Many also had a renewed desire to carry out "lone wolf" attacks—those that were planned and carried out without organized support.

Meanwhile, al Qaeda took the opportunity to quietly strengthen its own organization. In 2015, U.S. forces were shocked to discover a new al Qaeda training camp in Afghanistan. The terrorist organization also began a new recruitment campaign. It used the theme, "We are all Osama." In 2017, bin Laden's son Hamza issued a call for renewed attacks on America, saying, "I invite Muslims generally to take revenge on the Americans, the murderers of the Sheikh [bin Laden]."

Intelligence analysts cautioned that large-scale attacks by al Qaeda or other organizations couldn't be ruled out. But at the same time, they warned that the greatest threats to the U.S. and Europe in coming years would likely be homegrown violent extremists (HVEs). These people are not affiliated with a specific group but have encountered jihadi ideas and decided to carry out their own attacks. "What we have not been successful at is turning back the ideology," said congressman Adam Smith. "There are more people adhering to it now than there were [on September 11, 2001]."

Despite bin Laden's death, world leaders acknowledged that terrorism was a threat that wouldn't go away anytime soon. Fifteen years after 9/11, counterterrorism expert Bryan Price called terrorism "a chronic disease like cancer" and urged the world to see it not as a "threat that can be solved, defeated, or vanquished, but as an inevitable fact of modern life that can be managed and contained but never fully eliminated." His view makes it clear that, while bin Laden's death was a vital turning point in the war on terrorism, that struggle will continue well into the future.

1957	Osama bin Laden is born in Jeddah, Saudi Arabia, to a wealthy family.
1988	After helping to defeat the Soviets in Afghanistan, bin Laden forms al Qaeda to continue his jihad.
1992	Bin Laden moves to Sudan, and al Qaeda carries out its first attack, against a hotel in Yemen.
1995	The CIA forms the bin Laden unit to track bin Laden's background and activities.
1998	Bin Laden issues a public declaration of war against the U.S. in February; al Qaeda bombs U.S. embassies in Kenya and Tanzania on August 7.
October 12, 2000	Terrorists target the USS *Cole*, killing 17 American sailors.
September 11, 2001	Al Qaeda operatives crash four planes into the World Trade Center, the Pentagon, and a Pennsylvania field, killing 3,000.
October 7, 2001	The U.S. launches Operation Enduring Freedom after the Taliban refuses to turn over bin Laden.
December 2001	U.S. airstrikes and ground forces attack bin Laden's hideout at Tora Bora, but bin Laden escapes.
November 2002	Bin Laden issues an audiotape as proof that he is still alive.
July 2005	Al Qaeda attacks the London transportation system, killing 52 people.
2010	CIA analysts locate bin Laden's personal courier, Abu Ahmed al-Kuwaiti, and follow him to a compound in Abbottabad, Pakistan.
May 1–2, 2011	A U.S. Navy SEAL team raids the Abbottabad compound, killing bin Laden.
2014	A new terrorist organization, ISIL, takes over large parts of Iraq and Syria and declares itself a caliphate.
2017	Bin Laden's son Hamza calls for renewed attacks on America and the West.

caliphate—the chief Muslim civil and religious leader

coalition—an alliance or partnership of groups or countries

contingency—an event or emergency that may or may not occur, depending on circumstances and other events

DNA—the abbreviation for deoxyribonucleic acid, a substance in the body that carries genetic information; because each person's DNA is unique, DNA can be used in some cases to identify individuals or family members

drone—unmanned aircraft operated by remote control or computers; some drones carry video equipment or missiles

embassies—offices of government officials who are stationed in a foreign country

extremists—people who believe in using violence or other extreme measures to enforce uncompromising views

ideology—set of ideas and beliefs followed by an individual or group

Islamist—supporting a political ideology that seeks to obtain legitimacy from Islam but is instead opposed to the laws and values taught by that religion; the terms Islamism, political Islam, and Islamic fundamentalism are often used interchangeably

martyred—killed for one's beliefs, especially religious beliefs

Mullah Omar—Afghani militant who led the Taliban takeover of Afghanistan in the 1990s and ruled the country as emir from 1996 to 2001, when the Taliban was overthrown by U.S. forces; Omar died in 2013, but his death remained secret until 2015

Muslim—a follower of Islam, a religion that says there is one God—Allah—and that Muhammad is his prophet

Northern Alliance—the primary Afghan military coalition that resisted the Taliban and allied with U.S. forces to drive the Taliban from power in December 2001

Operation Enduring Freedom—the name for U.S. combat operations in Afghanistan, which began October 7, 2001; although the operation officially ended in December 2014, several thousand U.S. troops remained in Afghanistan to provide training and support to the Afghan military and government

Pentagon—the headquarters of the U.S. Department of Defense in Washington, D.C.; the five-story building is made up of concentric, five-sided rings

sharia—religious law based on the Koran and teachings of Muhammad that guides Islamic life; under sharia law, there is no separation of church and state

stealth—describing an aircraft design feature that uses wide angles to prevent the craft from being detected by radar

suicide vest—a vest wired with explosives and worn by an individual who intends to kill him- or herself and others by blowing it up

Taliban—a militant, conservative Islamic movement in Afghanistan that enforced harsh laws, such as excluding women from public life

The 9/11 Commission Report: Final Report of the National Commission on Terrorist Attacks upon the United States. Washington, D.C.: U.S. Government Printing Office, 2004.

Bergen, Peter L. *Manhunt: The Ten-Year Search for Bin Laden from 9/11 to Abbottabad.* New York: Crown, 2012.

————. *The Osama bin Laden I Know: An Oral History of al-Qaeda's Leader.* New York: Free Press, 2006.

Coll, Steve. *The Bin Ladens: An Arabian Family in the American Century.* New York: Penguin Press, 2008.

————. *Ghost Wars: The Secret History of the CIA, Afghanistan, and bin Laden, from the Soviet Invasion to September 10, 2001.* New York: Penguin Press, 2004.

O'Neill, Robert. *The Operator: Firing the Shots that Killed Osama bin Laden and My Years as a SEAL Team Warrior.* New York: Scribner, 2017.

Owen, Mark. *No Easy Day: The Autobiography of a Navy SEAL.* New York: Dutton, 2012.

Scott-Clark, Cathy, and Adrian Levy. *The Exile: The Stunning Inside Story of Osama bin Laden and Al Qaeda in Flight.* New York: Bloomsbury, 2017.

History: Osama bin Laden

https://www.history.com/topics/osama-bin-laden

This site presents a biography of Osama bin Laden, along with videos, speeches, and photos of the terrorist leader.

Navy SEAL Museum

https://www.navysealmuseum.org/

Learn more about Navy SEAL history, weapons, and operations.

Note: Every effort has been made to ensure that the websites listed above are suitable for children, that they have educational value, and that they contain no inappropriate material. However, because of the nature of the Internet, it is impossible to guarantee that these sites will remain active indefinitely or that their contents will not be altered.